GRUMPY CAT'S™ ROAD TRIP SPOT-THE-DIFFERENCES

John Kurtz

Dover Publications, Inc.
Mineola, New York

Copyright

Bibliographical Note

Grumpy Cat's Road Trip Spot-the-Differences is a new work,
first published by Dover Publications, Inc., in 2018.

International Standard Book Number

ISBN-13: 978-0-486-82470-3
ISBN-10: 0-486-82470-5

Manufactured in the United States by LSC Communications
82470501   2018
www.doverpublications.com

In this book, you'll find 27 spot-the-difference challenges featuring the internet's grumpy but lovable feline sensation. You'll join Grumpy Cat on a road trip across the USA to places such as Alcatraz in California, the Statue of Liberty in New York, and even a clown museum in Wisconsin. Even though the two renderings of each of the puzzles look the same, the image on the right side has been altered slightly to make it different from the original image on the left side. Can you help Grumpy Cat spot the changes in each puzzle? Try your best to find the differences, but if you get stuck, just turn to the Solutions section, which begins on page 56. When you are finished, you can color the pages to show Grumpy Cat's reaction to each of the places visited on this road trip.

"I'm in four states all at once and I'm not moving!"

Find and circle the 8 changes on this page.

"I tried holding my paw up so I look like Lady Liberty. Now I'm tired!"

Find and circle the 10 differences in this version.

"There's gold to be found in this mine. Do I look thrilled?"

There are 8 changes in this picture. Find and circle them.

"This prison tour is nothing to smile about.
I hope the guards don't mind my costume."

Find and circle the 7 differences in this picture.

"This big fish does not frown as well as I do.
Maybe I can give him lessons."

What's different on this page? Circle the 10 changes.

"Who says playing with twine is fun for cats? I'm feeling entangled."

Largest Ball of Twine

Take a close look and circle the 9 differences in this image.

"No way is a stalactite falling on my head!
I don't even know how to spell stalactite."

Help Grumpy Cat circle the 8 changes on this page.

"What are these clowns so happy about . . . I'm not laughing."

There are 10 changes on this page. Find and circle them.

"Hey, watch me snap the Delicate Arch!
(of course, I meant with my camera . . . not!)"

This image looks the same but it's not. Circle the 8 differences.

"Not fair! This donut isn't as big as advertised."

There are 8 changes in this picture. Find and circle them.

"Someone made me buy this terrible T-shirt.
Who loves the Sun anyway?"

Find and circle the 9 differences on this page.

"Who Says this Fun House is fun? I just scared myself."

Look for the 7 changes on this page and circle them.

"I saw a 630-foot arch over the Mississippi River once. It was awful."

There are 8 differences in this image. Find and circle them.

"Did I splatter some paint? Good."

Find and circle the 12 things that have changed in this picture.

"Another selfie coming up—one, two, nice big frown now!"

There are 8 changes on this page. Find and circle them.

"I've been famous for a long time—Hollywood is starting to annoy me!"

Can you spot the 9 differences on this page? Circle them.

"Did we really drive all this way for a picture in front of concrete?"

Find and circle 9 differences on this page.

FUN BALLOON RIDES

"When is the balloon ride over? I forgot my lunch."

Look for 9 differences on this page and circle them.

"Four score and seven years ago . . .
is when it seems like I started this book."

This image looks the same but it's not. Circle the 9 differences.

"I've had enough of this rainy weather!
Let me check out the Canadian Falls now."

There are 11 things that have changed on this page. Circle all of them.

"Okay, I'll wear this silly jester hat and the beads,
but NO! to the Mardi Gras parade."

Can you find the 7 changes on this page?

PLYMOUTH ROCK

"I came across the ocean once. All I found was a rock."

Find and circle the 9 differences in this picture.

"This geyser is really getting me steamed up!"

Search for 7 changes in this picture and circle them.

"If you're trying to look grumpier than I do, it's not working."

Look carefully at this picture and circle 9 changes.

49

"Washington, Jefferson, Roosevelt, Lincoln, Grumpy Cat—that's better!"

There are 9 changes on this page. Find and circle them.

"I said I wanted to go to space camp, not get sent into space!"

Find the 9 differences on this page and circle them.

"Who gave me this hat? It should say I ♥ trains."

There are 12 changes on this page. Find and circle them all.

Solutions

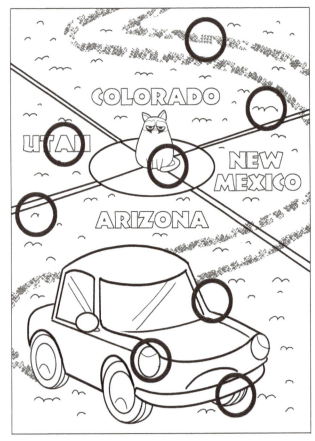

pages 2-3

pages 4-5

pages 6-7

pages 8-9

pages 10-11

pages 12-13

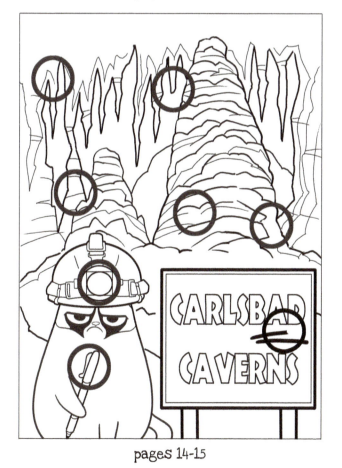

pages 14-15

pages 16-17

pages 18-19

pages 20-21

pages 22-23

pages 24-25

pages 26-27

pages 28-29

pages 30-31

pages 32-33

pages 34-35

pages 36-37

pages 38-39

pages 40-41

pages 42-43

PLYMOUTH ROCK

pages 44-45

pages 46-47

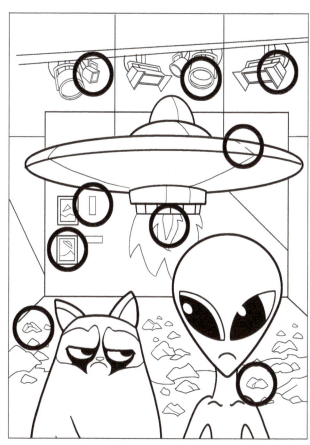

pages 48-49

pages 50-51

pages 52-53

pages 54-55